America's
ANIMAL
COMEBACKS

Black-footed Ferrets

Back from the Brink

by Miriam Aronin

Consultant: Dean E. Biggins, Ph.D.
U.S. Geological Survey (BRD)
Fort Collins Science Center

BEARPORT
PUBLISHING

New York, New York

Credits

Cover and Title Page, © Sumio Harada/Minden Pictures; 4–5, © LuRay Parker Wyoming Game and Fish Department; 7, © Tom McHugh/Photo Researchers, Inc.; 8, © Sumio Harada/Minden Pictures; 9, © Richard Reading/Denver Zoological Foundation; 10, © LuRay Parker/Wyoming Game and Fish Department; 11, © William Munoz; 12, © LuRay Parker/Wyoming Game and Fish Department; 13, © Robert E. Barber/Alamy; 14, © Lou Hanebury, U.S. Fish and Wildlife Service; 15, © Dean Biggins/U.S. Geological Survey; 16, © William Munoz; 17, © LuRay Parker/Wyoming Game and Fish Department; 18, © LuRay Parker/Wyoming Game and Fish Department; 19, © LuRay Parker/Wyoming Game and Fish Department; 20, © LuRay Parker/Wyoming Game and Fish Department; 21, © Richard Reading/Denver Zoological Foundation; 22, © Mike Lockhart/U.S. Fish and Wildlife Service; 22 Inset, © Mike Lockhart/U.S. Fish and Wildlife Service; 23, © Dean Biggins/U.S. Geological Survey; 24, © LuRay Parker/Wyoming Game and Fish Department; 26–27, © Sumio Harada/Minden Pictures; 28 © D. Robert Franz/Bruce Coleman, Inc; 29T, © Dr Vadim Sidorovich/Naturepl.com; 29B, © John Harold Castano.

Publisher: Kenn Goin
Editorial Director: Adam Siegel
Creative Director: Spencer Brinker
Photo Researcher: Beaura Kathy Ringrose
Cover Design: Dawn Beard Creative

Library of Congress Cataloging-in-Publication Data

Aronin, Miriam.
  Black-footed ferrets : back from the brink / by Miriam Aronin.
    p. cm. — (America's animal comebacks)
  Includes bibliographical references and index.
  ISBN-13: 978-1-59716-506-8 (library binding)
  ISBN-10: 1-59716-506-9 (library binding)
  1. Black-footed ferret—Juvenile literature. I. Title. II. Series.

  QL737.C25A764 2008
  599.76′629—dc22

                                  2007013404

For more information, write to Bearport Publishing Company, Inc., 101 Fifth Avenue, Suite 6R, New York, New York 10003. Printed in the United States of America.

10 9 8 7 6 5 4 3 2 1

Contents

A Thief in the Night

It was a cool night in Meeteetse (muh-TEET-see), Wyoming, on September 26, 1981. A dog named Shep wandered around the ranch where he lived. Suddenly, he spotted a strange creature stealing food from his bowl. Shep quickly attacked. He killed the animal and dragged it home.

Shep's owners, John and Lucille Hogg, had never seen anything like it. The dead animal had a long, thin body. The fur around its eyes was black and shaped like a mask. The tip of its tail and its legs were black, too.

The Hoggs showed the furry creature to an animal expert. He could hardly believe his eyes. Shep had found a black-footed ferret—an animal most people thought was **extinct**!

Black-footed ferrets are part of the weasel family. Other animals in this group include otters, wolverines, and skunks.

Black-footed ferrets are one of three kinds of ferrets in the world. They are the only kind that live in the wild in North America.

Long Ago in the West

Black-footed ferrets weren't always so **rare**. Until the 1800s, more than half a million of them lived on the American **prairies**. They ate, slept, and raised their young underground in **burrows** and tunnels. These burrows were dug by the ferrets' main **prey**—prairie dogs.

Black-footed Ferrets in the Wild

☐ Where ferrets lived before the 1800s
● Meeteetse, Wyoming

Prairie dogs and black-footed ferrets once lived throughout the American prairies. This map shows where ferrets lived before they began dying out.

In the late 1800s, farmers **settled** the American prairies. To them, prairie dogs were pests. These small animals ate the grass that farmers wanted for their cattle. So the farmers poisoned the prairie dogs. Millions were killed. When ferrets ate the poisoned prairie dogs, they also died in huge numbers. By 1967, it was almost impossible to find black-footed ferrets in the wild. The U.S. government listed the animal as **endangered**.

Before the 1800s, as many as five billion prairie dogs lived in North America. By the 1970s, people had destroyed more than 95 percent of the prairie dog **population**.

In the wild, prairie dogs make up 90 percent of the black-footed ferret's food.

New Hope

Between 1975 and 1980, many people believed black-footed ferrets were extinct. Nobody had seen one in the wild during that time. Then came Shep's big discovery in 1981.

Scientists hoped that more ferrets might still be living in Meeteetse. So they came to look for them. Finding ferrets, however, is not easy. The animals live mainly underground. They come up for short periods of time only to hunt or find a **mate**.

In the wild, black-footed ferrets spend 90 percent of their time underground.

On October 29, 1981, **biologist** Dennie Hammer got lucky. He spotted the first live ferret in the area. Hammer captured the animal and attached a tiny radio **transmitter**. When he let the ferret go, the transmitter would send out a signal. Scientists could now track the animal's movements.

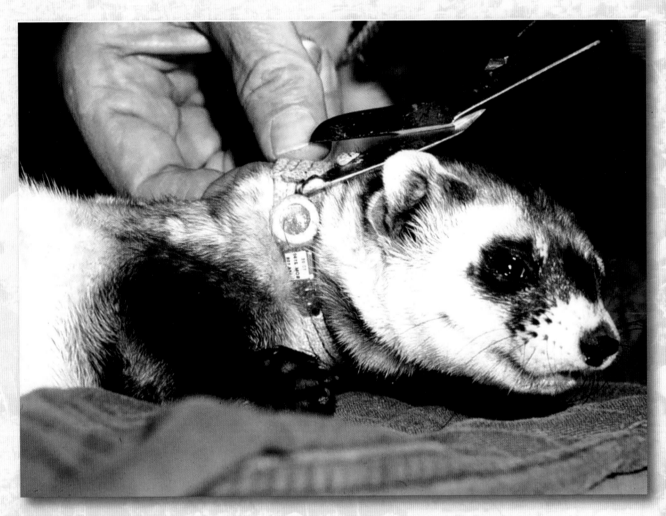

Biologists use radio transmitters, like the one on this ferret's collar, to track where animals go.

Disaster

Scientists continued searching Meeteetse for more ferrets. It was hard to find the animals. Ferrets usually only come out at night. So scientists set up spotlights. Now they could see the animals' eyes shining bright green in the dark.

Black-footed ferrets' eyes can **reflect** a high-power spotlight from about 655 feet (200 m) away.

In 1982, scientists counted 61 ferrets in Meeteetse. By 1984, they had found 129. However, in 1985 the number dropped to 58. Why were the furry creatures dying?

Biologists discovered that a disease called **plague** had killed thousands of prairie dogs around Meeteetse. The plague had spread to the ferrets and killed them, too. Ferrets were also dying from a disease called **canine distemper**. Scientists feared the animal would soon become extinct.

Scientists used tracks in the snow to help find the ferrets.

Captured!

To stop the ferrets from dying out, the government decided on a bold plan. Scientists would try to capture all the wild ferrets in Meeteetse! Then they could **breed** the ferrets in **captivity**.

It would not be easy. In the early 1970s, biologists had caught nine black-footed ferrets in South Dakota. They tried to breed them. Sadly, no babies survived.

A scientist captures a black-footed ferret.

Scientists would need to do a better job this time. From September 13 to October 12, 1985, they captured three male ferrets and three females. Unfortunately, two of the ferrets had canine distemper. Soon all the animals caught the deadly disease. There was no cure and they died.

Canine distemper is common in coyotes. Since they live near black-footed ferrets, coyotes may spread the deadly disease to them.

The Last Chance

By November 1985, scientists had captured six more ferrets to replace the ones that had died. This time, researchers made sure that none of the animals were sick.

Meanwhile, the number of ferrets in Meeteetse was falling fast. Between September and October 1985, the population had dropped from 31 to just 16 ferrets. By the summer of 1986, only four adults and their babies remained.

Dean Biggins is one of the scientists who helped rescue black-footed ferrets.

Scientists quickly rescued the animals. On March 1, 1987, they captured the very last wild ferret. Biologists now had just 18 healthy black-footed ferrets to breed. Would they be enough to save the **species**?

This female was one of the last black-footed ferrets in Meeteetse. She was captured in 1986.

The black-footed ferret is one of the most endangered **mammals** in North America.

New Kits

Scientists brought the ferrets from Meeteetse to the Sybille Wildlife Research Center in Wyoming for breeding. At first, the scientists were worried. None of the ferrets captured in 1985 had **kits** the following year. Luckily, two females gave birth to seven kits in 1987. The next year, 13 ferrets gave birth to 44 kits.

These kits are two weeks old.

Newborn ferret kits cannot walk. Their eyes are closed and they have no teeth. In the wild, black-footed ferret kits do not leave their burrows until they are about 60 days old.

By 1990, more than 120 black-footed ferrets were living in captivity. Biologists had started new breeding programs in Virginia, Nebraska, and Colorado. If the ferrets in one place became sick, the others would survive. All the captive ferrets were **descendants** of the Meeteetse group. Maybe someday they would live in the wild again.

A black-footed ferret kit born in captivity

Many Challenges

So far, breeding black-footed ferrets was a great success. Yet scientists still worried. What would happen when the animals were returned to the wild? Could they find enough food? Would they be able to stay safe from enemies?

These kits are 47 days old.

Scientists began looking for a good place to **reintroduce** the ferrets. The animals needed prairie dog burrows where they could live underground. There also had to be plenty of prairie dogs for the ferrets to eat. People nearby had to agree not to harm the ferrets or the prairie dogs. Finding the right place would not be easy.

To survive, a black-footed ferret must eat a prairie dog every three to four days. One black-footed ferret may eat more than 100 prairie dogs in a year.

Black-footed ferrets hunt prairie dogs—which are sometimes larger than the ferrets!

19

Return to the Wild

Scientists finally found a place where they hoped the ferrets could survive. In 1991, they reintroduced 49 black-footed ferrets in Shirley Basin, Wyoming.

Scientists watched the animals closely. In 1992, they got a hopeful sign. Two ferrets had kits. These were the first **litters** born in the wild since the Meeteetse ferrets were rescued!

Scientists used a special cage to release the ferrets in Shirley Basin, Wyoming.

The released ferrets faced deadly challenges, however. They were not used to hiding from **predators**. Many ferrets were killed by coyotes. Only a few kits survived from year to year. Scientists needed to find a way to help the creatures live on their own.

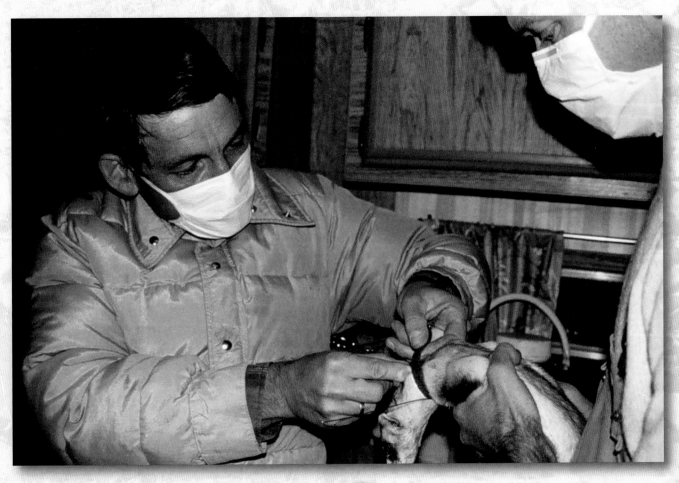

Scientists working with black-footed ferrets hope to breed and release enough captive ferrets so that 1,500 of them can live in ten different places in the wild.

Scientists placed radio collars on the ferrets so that they could find out what happened to some of the animals they released.

Learning to Survive

The ferrets bred in captivity had never lived in the wild. They weren't used to finding safety below the ground. Scientists realized the captive ferrets needed to learn survival skills. So they had them live in prairie dog burrows. The ferrets learned to survive underground before being released in the wild. The ferrets were given live prey, too. Now they could learn how to hunt.

Scientists set up burrows for the captive ferrets inside these protected pens. Prairie dogs were let loose in mounds of dirt to make the burrows.

Scientists also tested ways to teach ferrets to fear predators. They tried out their **experiments** on Siberian ferrets. The scientists flew a stuffed owl on a string. They put a badger skin on a remote-control toy truck. The ferrets weren't fooled, however.

The badger skin on the remote-control truck came to be known as the "Robo-badger."

Captive ferrets that are taught survival skills are ten times more likely to survive in the wild.

On the Right Track

Scientists saw that helping captive ferrets learn how to hunt and stay safe helped the furry creatures live in the wild. Soon all young black-footed ferrets were trained before being released. These ferrets survived longer than earlier groups.

The breeding programs were going well, too. In 1998, the ferrets produced 452 kits—a new record!

These ferrets were raised in pens before being released into the wild.

By 2002, scientists had reintroduced ferrets in six U.S. states. One group in South Dakota did very well. Those ferrets had so many kits that biologists decided to reintroduce some of them in Colorado. Unfortunately, disease forced some other places to end their programs.

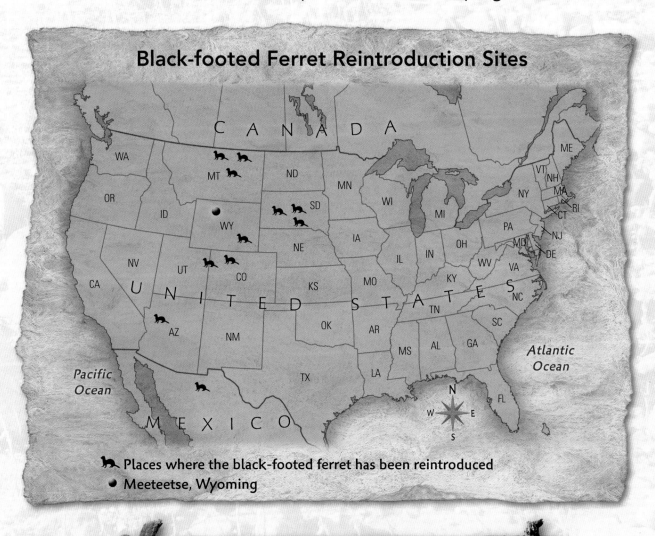

Black-footed Ferret Reintroduction Sites

🐾 Places where the black-footed ferret has been reintroduced
● Meeteetse, Wyoming

Countries in North America are working together to help black-footed ferrets. The Toronto Zoo in Canada has a breeding program, and ferrets have been reintroduced in Chihuahua, Mexico.

The Future

No one knows for sure if black-footed ferrets will make it. Not enough kits from reintroduced ferrets are surviving in the wild to save the species. Breeding programs need more money to continue. Also, there are few good **habitats** for ferrets in the wild.

More than 2,200 kits have been released into the wild since 1991.

Yet the future is promising. Since 1987, more than 5,000 kits have been born in captivity. The government already protects one kind of prairie dog. It may soon start protecting others. Then ferrets will have more food.

As biologist Mike Lockhart said, "Ferret recovery has been a huge success story." In just over 20 years, the world has gone from only 18 black-footed ferrets living in the wild to around 700.

Black-footed Ferret Facts

In 1973, Congress passed the Endangered Species Act. This law protects animals and plants that are in danger of dying out in the United States. Harmful activities, such as hunting, capturing, or collecting endangered species, are illegal under this act.

The black-footed ferret was one of the first species listed under the Endangered Species Act. Here are some other facts about the black-footed ferret.

Population: **North American population in the 1800s:**
probably between 500,000 and 1 million

North American population today:
about 700 in the wild; about 350 in captivity

Weight	Length	Food	Life Span
1.5–2.5 pounds (0.7–1.1 kg)	19–26 inches (48–66 cm), including tail	mainly prairie dogs, but sometimes mice, too	about 3–4 years in the wild

Fur Color
brownish-yellow, with white fur on the sides of the head, and around the mouth and nose; a black "mask" around the eyes, black feet and legs, and black at the tip of the tail

Original Habitat
short-grass and middle-grass prairies on the American Great Plains, from southern Canada to northern Mexico

28

Other Weasel Family Members in Danger

The black-footed ferret is one kind of animal in the weasel family that's making a comeback by increasing its numbers. Other animals in this family are also trying to make a comeback.

European Mink

- European mink once lived throughout Europe and western Asia.

- In the 1900s, American mink raised on farms in Europe escaped. They started taking over the European mink's habitat.

- Today, European mink live only in France, Spain, and other isolated places in eastern Europe and western Asia.

- Scientists are trying to save the European mink by breeding it in captivity. They are also releasing European mink on islands that the American mink cannot reach.

Colombian Weasel

- The Colombian weasel is one of the rarest animals in South America.

- By 1996, only five Colombian weasels had ever been seen.

- The Colombian weasel lives in the countries of Colombia and Ecuador.

- Colombian weasels have been found between 5,741 feet (1,750 m) and 8,858 feet (2,700 m) above sea level.

Glossary

biologist (bye-OL-uh-jist) a scientist who studies plants or animals

breed (BREED) to produce young

burrows (BUR-ohz) tunnels or holes in the ground made by animals, such as prairie dogs

canine distemper (KAY-nine diss-TEMP-ur) a deadly disease that can infect dogs and other animals, causing fever and loss of appetite

captivity (kap-TIV-uh-tee) being held in a place where one cannot escape

descendants (di-SEND-uhnts) people or animals that come from a family that lived earlier in time

endangered (en-DAYN-jurd) being in danger of dying out

experiments (ek-SPER-uh-ments) scientific tests set up to find answers to questions

extinct (ek-STINGKT) when a kind of plant or animal has died out; no more of its kind is living anywhere in the world

habitats (HAB-uh-*tats*) places in nature where a plant or animal normally lives

kits (KITS) baby ferrets; short for "kittens"

litters (LIT-urz) all of the young born at the same time to an animal

mammals (MAM-uhlz) warm-blooded animals that have a backbone, hair or fur on their skin, and drink their mothers' milk as babies

mate (MATE) one of a pair of animals that breed together

plague (PLAYG) a deadly disease that is spread by fleas and rodents, such as mice and prairie dogs

population (*pop*-yuh-LAY-shuhn) the total number of a kind of animal living in a place

prairies (PRAIR-eez) large areas of flat land covered with grass

predators (PRED-uh-turz) animals that hunt other animals for food

prey (PRAY) animals that are hunted or caught for food

rare (RAIR) not often found or seen

reflect (ri-FLEKT) to bounce back light

reintroduce (*ree*-in-truh-DOOSS) to return animals to the wild

settled (SET-uhld) made a home and lived in a new place

species (SPEE-sheez) groups that animals are divided into, according to similar characteristics; members of the same species can have offspring together

transmitter (tranz-MIT-ur) a device that sends out radio waves to help scientists track an animal

Bibliography

Brady, Jeff. "Black-Footed Ferrets Fight Extinction," *Morning Edition*, NPR (September 26, 2006). Online at **www.npr.org/templates/story/story. php?storyId=6140397.**

Hawes, Alex. "Black-Footed Ferrets: Life Behind the Mask," *ZooGoer*, vol. 29. no. 5 (September/October 2000). Online at **http://nationalzoo. si.edu/publications/zoogoer/2000/5/blackfootedferrets.cfm.**

Miller, Brian, Richard P. Reading, and Steve Forrest. *Prairie Night: Black-Footed Ferrets and the Recovery of Endangered Species.* Washington, D.C.: Smithsonian Institution Press (1996).

Silverstein, Alvin and Virginia, and Laura Silverstein Nunn. *The Black-Footed Ferret.* Brookfield, CT: The Millbrook Press (1995).

Read More

Hirschi, Ron. *Where Are My Prairie Dogs and Black-Footed Ferrets?* New York: Bantam Books (1992).

Johnson, Sylvia A. *Ferrets.* Minneapolis, MN: Carolrhoda Books (1997).

Nirgiotis, Nicholas and Theodore. *No More Dodos: How Zoos Help Endangered Wildlife.* Minneapolis, MN: Lerner Publications (1996).

Patent, Dorothy Hinshaw. *Prairie Dogs.* New York: Clarion Books (1993).

Learn More Online

To learn more about black-footed ferrets and their return to the wild, visit **www.bearportpublishing.com/AnimalComebacks**

Index

About the Author

Miriam Aronin is a writer and editor. She also enjoys reading, knitting, and visiting endangered species at the zoo.